Happy Holidays!

Martin Luther King, Jr. Day

by Betsy Rathburn

BELLWETHER MEDIA
MINNEAPOLIS, MN

BLASTOFF!
Beginners

Blastoff! Beginners are developed by literacy experts and educators to meet the needs of early readers. These engaging informational texts support young children as they begin reading about their world. Through simple language and high frequency words paired with crisp, colorful photos, Blastoff! Beginners launch young readers into the universe of independent reading.

Blastoff! Universe

Reading Level — Grade K

Grades 1-3

BLASTOFF! DISCOVERY — Grade 4

Sight Words in This Book 🔍

a	he	it	this
about	help	other	to
be	his	people	up
day	in	the	was
for	is	they	we

This edition first published in 2023 by Bellwether Media, Inc.

No part of this publication may be reproduced in whole or in part without written permission of the publisher. For information regarding permission, write to Bellwether Media, Inc., Attention: Permissions Department, 6012 Blue Circle Drive, Minnetonka, MN 55343.

Library of Congress Cataloging-in-Publication Data

Names: Rathburn, Betsy, author.
Title: Martin Luther King, Jr. Day / by Betsy Rathburn.
Description: Minneapolis, MN : Bellwether Media, Inc., 2023. | Series: Blastoff! Beginners: Happy holidays! | Includes bibliographical references and index. | Audience: Ages 4-7 years | Audience: Grades K-1
Identifiers: LCCN 2022036389 (print) | LCCN 2022036390 (ebook) | ISBN 9798886871036 (Library Binding) | ISBN 9798886871913 (Paperback) | ISBN 9798886872293 (eBook)
Subjects: LCSH: Martin Luther King, Jr., Day--Juvenile literature.
Classification: LCC E185.97.K5 R37 2023 (print) | LCC E185.97.K5 (ebook) | DDC 394.261--dc23/eng/20220805
LC record available at https://lccn.loc.gov/2022036389
LC ebook record available at https://lccn.loc.gov/2022036390

Editor: Christina Leaf   Designer: Laura Sowers

Printed in the United States of America, North Mankato, MN.

Table of Contents

It Is Martin Luther King, Jr. Day!

We help people in need.
It is Martin Luther King, Jr. Day!

A Great Leader

This holiday
is in January.
It is the
third Monday.

It honors Martin Luther King, Jr. He was a great leader.

Martin Luther King, Jr.

He fought for **civil rights**. He wanted everyone to be **equal**.

A DAY ON... NOT A DAY OFF

REMEMBER! CELEBRATE! ACT!

MARTIN LUTHER
KING JR.

Learning and Helping

People learn about Martin Luther King, Jr.

They listen to
his ideas.

People help others.
They give money.
Volunteers
give food.

volunteers

17

People **march**. They stand up for Martin's ideas!

march

We honor a
great leader.
We work
to change
the world!

Martin Luther King, Jr. Day Facts

Celebrating Martin Luther King, Jr. Day

volunteer

food

Martin Luther King, Jr. Day Activities

learn about Martin

help others

march

Glossary

civil rights

rights in government that every person should have

equal

the same as others

march

to walk to support an idea

volunteers

people who help others for free

To Learn More

ON THE WEB

FACTSURFER

Factsurfer.com gives you a safe, fun way to find more information.

1. Go to www.factsurfer.com.

2. Enter "Martin Luther King, Jr. Day" into the search box and click 🔍.

3. Select your book cover to see a list of related content.

Index

The images in this book are reproduced through the courtesy of: Julie Clopper, cover; LightField Studios, p. 3; Jeffrey Isaac Greenberg 9+/ Alamy, pp. 4-5; Jeffrey Isaac Greenberg 12+/ Alamy, pp. 6-7, 12-13; Phil Stanziola/ Wikipedia, p. 8 (Martin Luther King, Jr.); EPG_EuroPhotoGraphics, pp. 8-9, 23 (march); Frances Robert/ Alamy, pp. 10-11; Jeffrey Isaac Greenberg 11+/ Alamy, pp. 14-15; Rob Kim/ Stringer/ Getty Images, pp. 16-17; Danny Raustadt, pp. 18-19; Tim Brown/ Alamy, pp. 20-21; NG Images/ Alamy, p. 22 (celebrating); wavebreakmedia, p. 22 (learn about Martin); Dmytro Zinkevych, p. 22 (help others); Xavier Ascanio, p. 22 (march); Rowland Scherman/ Wikipedia, p. 23 (civil rights); Aerial Mike, p. 23 (equal); Ground Picture, p. 23 (volunteers).